EXPERIMENTS IN REFLECTION

EXPERIMENTS IN REFLECTION

How to See the Present, Reconsider the Past, and Shape the Future

Leticia Britos Cavagnaro

Illustrations by Gabriela Sánchez

TEN SPEED PRESS
California | New York

HASSO PLATTNER
Institute of Design at Stanford

Contents

A Note from the d.school vii

Introduction 1

COLLECTION ONE
Notice 13

EXPERIMENT #1
Get in the Mood for Reflection 15
*Noticing your moods improves your
ability to learn from your experiences
and make decisions.*

EXPERIMENT #2
Shift Gears 23
*Slowing down your pace bumps
up your awareness.*

EXPERIMENT #3
See What Matters 31
*Using different lenses to direct your
attention brings unexpected insights
into focus.*

EXPERIMENT #4
Figure Out Who You Are, Really 41
*Exploring who you are and how
others see you shapes your decisions
and actions.*

COLLECTION TWO
Make Sense 51

EXPERIMENT #5
Make Your Thinking Visible 53
*Visualizing relationships between
thoughts and ideas trains your brain
to make better connections.*

EXPERIMENT #6
Find Questions to Your Answers 63
*Seeking questions instead of answers
takes you to a new territory worth
exploring.*

EXPERIMENT #7
Climb the Ladder of Meaning 71
*Exploring multiple levels of abstraction
helps you discover what really matters
and better ways to get there.*

EXPERIMENT #8
**Travel through the Wormholes
of Reflection 79**
*Creating metaphors transports you to
different universes of meaning.*

COLLECTION THREE
Envision 87

EXPERIMENT #9
Reflect Forward 89
Imagining a multitude of possible futures allows you to steer toward the one you aspire to create.

EXPERIMENT #10
Build Futures You Can Touch 97
Reimagining everyday objects activates your ability to conceive possible futures.

EXPERIMENT #11
Don't Finish What You Sta . . . 105
Thinking about what you could start instead of what you need to finish helps you plant seeds for a better future for the generations to come.

EXPERIMENT #12
Be a Good Ancestor 115
Connecting with the inhabitants of the future helps you think differently about your decisions and contribute to intergenerational justice.

**Reflecting on Reflection
and Becoming a Reflective
Practitioner 122**
An Insight-o-Meter Logbook 129
Sources and Resources 130
Grateful Reflections 131
Index 134

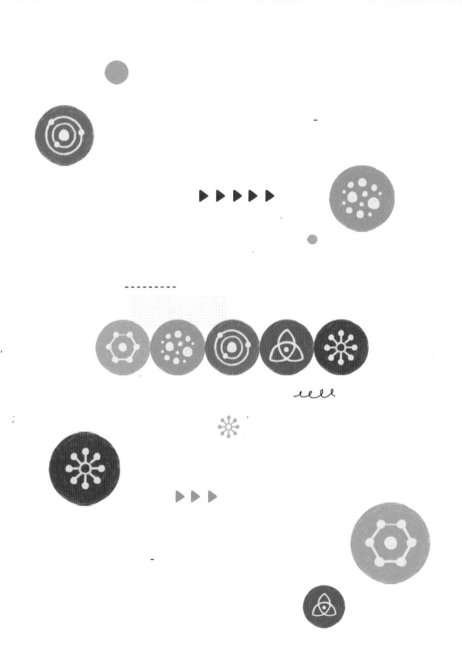

A Note from the d.school

At the Stanford d.school, *design* is a verb. It's an attitude
to embody and a way to work. The core of that work is
trying, to the best of one's abilities, to help things run more
smoothly, delight more people, and ease more suffering.
This holds true for you, too—whether design is your
profession or simply a mindset you bring to life.

Founded in 2005 as a home for wayward thinkers, the
d.school was a place where independent-minded people
could gather, try out ideas, and make change. A lot has
shifted in the decade or so since, but that original exuberant
and resourceful attitude is as present today as it was then.

Our series of guides is here to offer you the same
inventiveness, insight, optimism, and perseverance that
we champion at the d.school. Like a good tour guide, these
handbooks will help you find your way through unknown
territory and introduce you to some fundamental ideas
that we hope will become cornerstones in your creative
foundation.

Celebrate your unique perspective and uncover the tools of
change-making in *Design Social Change*. Bring your ideas to
life with *Make Possibilities Happen*. And in this book, learn
to get in tune with yourself and the world around you.

Welcome to *Experiments in Reflection*!

love,
the d.school

Introduction

"Let me reflect on that" is a common phrase that you've probably said (or heard) more than once. And it's a saying that seemingly doesn't need to be explained. You wanted some time to think about "that," whatever "that" was. But what did you mean, really, by *reflect*? Are thinking and reflecting the same thing?

This book is an invitation to reconsider not only what reflection is, but also how incorporating reflection into your life can help you find meaning in your experiences, make better decisions, and shape a path toward your aspirations.

If reflection is the *what* of this book, experiments are the *how*.

I am a professional experimenter. After doing my fair share of school science experiments, I pursued a career as a scientist. I spent a couple of decades in a biology lab and got a doctorate in developmental biology. When I transitioned to the field of education, I discovered that the experimental mindset I had acquired was a superpower when it came to learning pretty much anything. As an educator and leader at Stanford's Hasso Plattner Institute of Design (aka the d.school), my latest experimental endeavors have been focused on finding better ways to teach and learn—and reflection is a key component of my methods.

The experimentation in scientific studies advance our collective knowledge in different fields. But experimentation also drives learning in our day-to-day lives—think of a baby throwing food from their highchair to see what happens, a home cook tweaking a recipe until it's perfect, or someone trying out different ways to communicate with a loved one.

For this reason, I've crafted a set of experiments for this book, organized into three collections, so that you can put into practice a range of reflection methods. Doing experiments may sound complicated and time-consuming, and you might be tempted to just read the book and skip the doing part. Yes, by reading, you'll learn something— maybe a lot—about reflection, but don't settle for that! I don't want you to just *learn about* reflection. I want you to *become* a (more) reflective human, and an experimenter too. Doing the experiments helps you get out of your head and into the world (even if you don't physically step outside). That's when you stretch your reflection muscles the most. At the same time, working through this book shouldn't feel like a chore. Try those experiments that speak to you and skip the ones that don't (you can always come back to them later).

A Nondefinitive
Definition of Reflection

I see reflection as **a whole-body process of transforming experience into meaning to shape the future**. Let's unpack the components of this way of looking at reflection.

Whole-body process. Our brain gets most of the credit when we talk about thinking or learning. The credit is well deserved, as the brain does much of the heavy lifting, but in reality, the brain works with the whole body. The visual cortex of the brain receiving signals from our eyes is just one example. When it comes to reflection, the brain functions as a connector—it integrates external and internal signals captured through our senses, the networks of neurons that represent our existing knowledge, and the motor areas that trigger actions like moving or speaking. The first collection of experiments I share in this book (see pages 13–49) are dedicated to amplifying the ways in which we experience the world through our senses.

Transforming experience into meaning. Our experiences make up our world. And there is no one world that we all live in. Each of us navigates many worlds that we construct and reconstruct. Our concrete experiences— like reading this book or interacting with people—are the raw materials. Reflection allows us to sculpt those raw materials into structures of meaning that support our goals and shape our values. The second collection of experiments (see pages 51–85) will lead you to explore reflection as a catalyst for creating meaning from your personal experiences.

Shape the future. Like reflection, the future is such a familiar concept that we may not think much about it. After all, we are continuously moving into the future, whether we want to or not: the next minute, the next day, the next year. And while we usually associate reflection with the past, reflecting on the future is not only possible but also necessary. In fact, what lies ahead of us is not a single future, but multiple possible futures.

As in a chess game, at any given moment, you may make decisions that open different paths. Naturally, some decisions are more consequential than others, but this basic fact remains: by reflecting on our present decisions and the possible futures they may unlock, we go from accidental future travelers to purposeful future shapers.

And when we embrace the plurality of the word *futures*, we can also recognize that many of our actions and decisions affect other people. Being mindful of this power and privilege invites us to build futures that benefit a more diverse group of people. The third collection of experiments (see pages 87–121) invites you to test the future-shaping power of reflection.

What You Need

For most of these experiments you just need a pen and paper. It's important to capture your work, so I recommend getting a notebook that you can use as you work through the experiments and can refer back to later. If an experiment requires more than just pen and paper, I call it out at the start. All of the experiments can be done in a short amount of time—from twenty minutes to an hour—but you can extend any part of them. I also offer a few follow-up experiments to go deeper.

You can do these experiments by yourself. In fact, I urge you to do them by yourself. When we try new things, the fear of being judged by others can get in the way. In these *private* experiments, no one will see your thoughts and ideas (unless you choose to share them). Take full advantage of this. Give yourself permission to explore with authentic curiosity and go to uncomfortable places. This is where you'll learn the most.

The Anatomy of an Experiment

Each experiment starts with a hypothesis to test. Simply put, a hypothesis is a statement that I offer as a starting point for learning. With each experiment, you will test how the hypothesis works in your own context. You may gather data that supports it or challenges it. Either result is valid.

After making sure you have the necessary materials, read the complete set of instructions laid out in the method and then follow them step by step.

Do First

I don't give you a lot of background information *before* you dive into each method. This is intentional. I want you to try the experiment and gather your own data before you consider what research shows and other people say. Otherwise, you may discount what your direct experience evokes because it doesn't fit into those insights.

As you run your experiment, you may wonder at times, *Am I doing it right?* The answer to this is always: *Yes! You are doing it right because you are doing it!* Some of the activities might feel artificial, and that's also by design. As a basketball player, I do drills during practice that look like nothing I may do during a real game; for instance, dribble with two balls. These artificial movements isolate and stretch specific abilities. You will do the equivalent with some of these experiments. Before we continue exploring the anatomy of an experiment, I invite you to get your gears in motion with this quick active reflection:

A Three-Minute Tactile Reflection

1 Find a sheet of paper or rip out the page of a notebook.

2 Crumple it.

3 Then flatten it.

4 Look at the lines and creases in the paper and the shapes they form. Notice how the light reflects on them. Move the paper around. Look at both sides.

5 Feel the texture. Do this with your eyes closed.

Now consider:
What did this sensory exploration evoke for you?
What did you notice?
What parallels can you draw with *the way you pay attention* to the environment, people, and events you encounter daily?

What might you try in the future to notice more?

Use what you have to activate the power of reflection— start now!

Assess Your Results

Once you have run each experiment, turn to the "Assess Your Results" section to make sense of your data. Use the following insight-o-meter to gauge your results.

The insight-o-meter is a simple rubric to help you evaluate how the experiment worked for you. If the reflection method helped you figure out something you had not realized before, then you may have gotten to the *Aha!* territory.

Hmm . . .
Maybe there is something there. I just need to think more about it.

Meh.
This method did nothing for me. I didn't uncover anything interesting.

Aha!
I uncovered a new way of thinking about something.

INSIGHT-O-METER

Another way to put it: the experiment helped you "connect the dots." Insights are new perspectives that can inform your decisions and actions. They may seem obvious in retrospect but are surprising the first time they come to mind. If an experiment doesn't seem to reveal any insights, then you would assess the outcome as *Meh*, and that's okay. You didn't do anything wrong; there are no guaranteed results with experiments. Maybe this was not the right method for you right now. If you are on the fence about whether you have realized something you didn't know before, then you may mark your result as *Hmm* . . . This can be an invitation to step away and come back later. A period of incubation may help your brain do the final push and find some interesting connections.

Capture your insight-o-meter data for each experiment in your notebook. It may be useful to look back at this information later and search for patterns across experiments too. While getting a life-changing insight will not happen every time you reflect, building a reflective practice drastically ups the odds in your favor. Also, insights tend to morph and recombine, and the more you gather, the more chances you create for that to happen.

As part of the process of writing this book, I invited a group of people to join what I call the Reflection Lab. They ran these same experiments, and I share insights from them throughout the book so that you can learn from the perspectives of others too.

The Experimenter's Pledge

In your journey as a reader and experimenter, it is important to establish norms that will get you in the right mindset to try new things and maximize your learning. I do this in all of the courses I teach, by asking my students—who could be undergraduates, professors, or even company executives—to agree to a set of norms. They will be trying ways of learning and working that may be unfamiliar and, in some cases, even uncomfortable. Recognizing this and agreeing on shared commitments create a safe environment in which to try them.

In a recent workshop, my co-instructor, sam seidel, invited students to be *vulnerageous*—a combination of *vulnerable* and *courageous*. Being vulnerageous became one of the shared agreements in a pledge that the class committed to. Other norms that contribute to setting the stage for learning might be: *I will be inclusive of the perspectives of others*, *I will make others look good* (because they will make me look good in return), and *I will use failure as a springboard for learning*. The complete set of norms— what I call the Experimenter's Pledge—varies according to the composition and goals of each group.

I invite you to craft your own Experimenter's Pledge. Here's one norm to get you started: *I will accept that my experiments may yield more questions than answers.*

This is based on a basic tenet of how experiments work: There is no such thing as a failed experiment. I've come to realize that I learned much more from those experiments that yielded perplexing or confusing results. Though my first instinct at the time was to label those experiments as failures, turning the results into new questions was far more valuable than any definitive answer because it illuminated new directions for inquiry. Here are a few other norms that I've found to be helpful and that you could include in your pledge: *I will get off autopilot, I will show up with my whole self, I will give myself permission to try new things.* Now add a few more of your own if you'd like.

You don't need to be fully on board with these commitments just yet or know exactly how to put them into practice. Just give them a try and, as you work your experimentation muscles with this book, come back to your Experimenter's Pledge now and then to renew—or revisit—your commitments.

Now let's be vulnerageous and dive in!

Notice

Reflection can be a tool of awareness. This first collection of experiments aims to develop your ability to be present and focus your attention. Try these experiments when you sense the need to center yourself in the present moment and heighten your capacity to notice important details.

Get in the Mood for Reflection

While it may seem like your moods can get in the way of seeing things clearly, tuning in to them allows you to better navigate your experiences and understand yourself. Focus your attention on your moods to learn more about how you respond to different situations and people, and why.

Hypothesis

The first time I tried stand-up paddleboarding, the water was pretty calm, but I kept falling off the board almost as soon as I got on it. I could feel the clouds of frustration moving in, but I persevered, and after a while, they dissipated. Feeling the warmth of confidence setting in in their place, I started to enjoy the moment and could focus on learning new moves.

Moods behave like an emotional weather system, bringing in storm fronts of anger and calming winds of joy. We sense moods in our body as we do emotions. But unlike emotions, which are usually directed at a particular person or situation, moods appear in more diffuse forms. So you may not always be aware of what mood you are in, and this is where you can get into trouble. Moods often affect your decisions and actions; they can also influence how others react to you and contribute to establishing the culture of the teams and organizations you belong to—for good or bad.

In this experiment you will test the hypothesis that **noticing your moods improves your ability to learn from your experiences and make decisions**.

Method

1. In your notebook, jot down a recent event that you would like to understand better. Note particular moments from that event that stand out to you; for instance, when a teammate shared feedback with you, or an awkward period of silence after you shared an idea with someone.

2. From the following two lists, select the moods you detected in yourself during the moments you wrote down.

List I
frustration, anxiety, confusion, skepticism, boredom, resignation, overwhelm, impatience

List II
ambition, confidence, perplexity, inquiry, trust, resolution, wonder, prudence

3. Consider the moods you detected. Did you select lots of moods or very few to none? How might they help you make sense of the event?

Reflect

▶ Use the insight-o-meter (see page 8) to gauge your insights before you move to the following page.

✹ ✹ Assess Your Results

The two lists of moods just offered can be characterized as "unproductive" and "productive" moods, respectively.

Unproductive moods get in the way of learning from your experiences and progressing toward your goals. Productive moods, on the other hand, predispose you to learn and support you in achieving your goals. For instance, in the face of a situation we don't understand, we may fall into a mood of confusion that makes us interpret our not knowing as a bad thing. A mood of wonder, on the other hand, pairs the not knowing with a sense of excitement about figuring it out.

In your experiment, the balance of productive to unproductive moods may have gone in one direction or another, and that's a valuable observation to reflect on. It is also possible that you were able to detect very few or even no moods when thinking of the situation you wanted to understand better. This could be interpreted in a few different ways. It may be that too much time has passed and the visceral memory of the experience has faded. But it is also possible that your moods sensor has yet to be attuned. Noticing your moods takes practice, as does developing what psychology professor Lisa Feldman Barrett calls "emotional granularity," or the ability to put feelings into words.

Being aware of your moods can expose hot spots that are worth exploring. This is especially true of unproductive moods. Just as thunderstorms are caused by the collision of warm moist air with cold air, moods can be the manifestation of our beliefs colliding with reality. When we have strong beliefs about what should and should not happen in a situation, those beliefs can often be at odds with what does happen or even with what we think is possible. For example, if you find yourself feeling impatient when a collaborator doesn't do something to your satisfaction, you may have the following beliefs:

Only *I* can do things that meet my standards.

There is no point in delegating anything, because in the end I will have to do it myself.

The beliefs underlying our moods can be explicit—that is, they are out in the open and we talk about them—or implicit and not apparent to others (and often to ourselves). Whether explicit or implicit, our beliefs affect how we interpret our experiences and guide our actions.

To dig a layer deeper as you examine any hot spots marked by moods, ask yourself what evidence you have to support your beliefs. In many cases you may find that you came to a belief based on an automatic response—a learned reaction to past experiences that is no longer serving you well.

Becoming aware of moods is the first step. Learning to shift from unproductive to productive moods is where you'll realize the full value of this reflection method. What if, when faced with what you see as unsatisfactory work by a collaborator, you cultivate a mood of inquiry instead of impatience, asking yourself questions such as, *What is getting in the way of this colleague performing this task well?,* or *Are we on the same page about what a satisfactory result looks like?* This might help you reframe your beliefs and ultimately allow you to act differently; for instance, inviting your collaborator to have a conversation about what good work looks like for each of you or helping them to identify improvement opportunities.

This experiment was inspired by my collaboration with the learning and development organization Pluralistic Networks' cofounder Gloria Flores and her extensive work in the area of learning to learn. One strategy Gloria uses to help people work more effectively in teams is to create challenges within the online role-playing game *World of Warcraft.* I experienced this firsthand, working alongside a team of four other people I had met only inside this virtual world. We had to tackle a series of increasingly difficult quests that revealed how our moods affected our ability to work together. As Gloria describes in her book, *Learning to Learn and the Navigation of Moods,* the challenges in the game parallel those we encounter in real life. For instance, one key insight came for me when a virtual teammate mentioned how my reading of the mission instructions out loud for all to hear had interrupted the flow of the game. When I realized that this feedback resulted in a mood of confusion and frustration (*I don't understand! I'm only trying to help us complete the mission!*), I examined the beliefs underlying these moods (Did I not trust my teammates to keep track of the tasks?). Then I shifted to a mood of wonder by asking myself how I could be more mindful of when to speak up and when to go with the flow and trust that the game would reveal the next steps. I also realized that this experience paralleled the real-life scenario of designing and running large events for students in my program. Through my being intentional about the level of detail and especially the timing of communicating those details to my teammates, the team and I both feel less anxiety, which results in a better experience for all.

Becoming aware of your moods is the main goal of this experiment. **As you go about your day, practice pausing now and then to identify what mood you are in.** If you further reflect on your underlying beliefs, you can adjust course, cultivate productive moods to replace unproductive ones, and take actions that are more likely to lead to desired outcomes.

Shift Gears

When you move fast to get to where you need to go, you miss opportunities to discover what the path has to offer. If you slow down, you may discover an entirely different destination worth visiting.

Hypothesis

The last time I had to leave my car at the mechanic's for repairs, I decided on impulse to walk back home. I estimated it might take me about thirty minutes to walk the mile-and-a-half stretch, and I set out at a brisk pace. A couple of blocks later, the iconic steep hills of San Francisco made me slow down. A lot. Increasingly out of breath, for a moment I worried that it would take me much longer than I had calculated to get home. Then I realized that I had nothing on my schedule for the rest of the morning. Why was I rushing in the first place? I also realized I had barely paid attention to my surroundings.

As we go about our daily routines, we often slip into autopilot mode, and the compelling needs to get to where we are going and be efficient set us on a fast pace. Moving slowly feels like a waste of time. In this experiment I invite you to challenge the assumption that fast is always better and to test how **slowing down your pace bumps up your awareness**.

Method

1. Identify a route that you normally take to get to work, home, the gym, or your favorite coffee shop. Regardless of how you normally travel on this route— car, bike, public transit, or walking—your mission is to walk this stretch (or part of it) *as slowly as you can*.

2. As you walk, pay attention to as many details as possible. What do you notice that you haven't noticed before? It may be a whole building you didn't realize was there, or small cracks on the sidewalk.

3. When you are back from your walk, take notes about all the new things you observed.

4. Identify a few tasks from your daily routine that you normally rush through. This could be breakfast with your family or a weekly work meeting—check your daily calendar for ideas. The next time you do that task, practice slowing down and make an effort to be in the moment instead of mentally racing to the next thing on the calendar.

Reflect

▶ Use the insight-o-meter (see page 8) to gauge your insights before you move to the following page.

✺ ✺ Assess Your Results

Scientists from the Memory and Aging Center at the University of California, San Francisco, studied the effects of fifteen-minute "awe walks." They found that people who received instructions to cultivate awe as they walk, pay attention to details, and observe with fresh, childlike eyes reported significantly higher levels of well-being.

One of the first things I noticed on my slow walk back from the mechanic's was the power of habits. There were many walking routes I could have taken, yet I ended up walking in a straight line down the same one-way street I'm used to taking while driving home from Stanford. This made me reflect on the automatic ways I tend to react in certain situations.

Once I started zigzagging up other side streets on the rest of my way home, I made a few interesting discoveries: I found an exuberant city park I had never noticed, just a few blocks from my apartment. I also noticed several creative ways of expressing values and ideas in windows, on door mats, and with garden decorations. This made me reflect on what might be equivalent ways in which I could display my values and passions for others to discover.

As you reflect on your experiment, **consider what side-road adventures you might be missing by always moving in a straight path**.

During my walk I was forced to slow down when I started walking up a hill, and that's when I started noticing more things. Translating this to my everyday routine, I asked myself, *What might be the equivalent to a steep hill?* One strategy that works for me is to restart my computer in the middle of the day so I have to wait for a few minutes and do nothing. Even the short time it takes for the computer to reboot is an opportunity to slow down (if I resist scrolling through the inbox on my phone, that is!). **Where can you add friction to create slow moments in your routine so you can be present and notice more?**

FOLLOW-UP EXPERIMENTS

Create space to go slow. Look at your calendar to spot commitments that fall at the intersection of these two criteria: (1) you are not really looking forward to it and (2) you are not an essential attendee (at least question the assumption that you are). Consider ways to eliminate these commitments by changing either the *who* (finding someone who could take your place) or the *how* (for instance, transforming a working meeting with a colleague into a collaborative document in which you both can work asynchronously).

Hack your to-do list. In addition to the appointments in your calendar, the items that pile up on your to-do list also contribute to the perception that you need to move fast. Take a moment to assess what's on your to-do list, and move some of those items to a *not*-to-do list as a way to actively decelerate. You can use the same criteria suggested for the previous follow-up experiment to decide which items could be moved to that list.

Build incubation periods. Schedule the times you will work on a given project, but also schedule times to intentionally step away from the work. Your brain's capacity to work in the background can yield unexpected connections. Kick off these incubation periods by actively focusing your attention on the issue or idea you are working on for just a few minutes. Then go for a walk or fold clothes or take a shower. Any automatic activity that doesn't require your focused attention will do. Sleep works too!

See What Matters

What does it mean to pay attention to something? If you broaden your definition of *attention*, you can learn interesting things about your ability to focus on those elements that will help you gain a new perspective on a situation.

Hypothesis

"Pay attention!" We all likely heard this admonition in school from an early age. At this command, we were supposed to sit still and fixate our eyes on the board or book in front of us, as if unrelenting focus would help us see what the teacher wanted us to see. As it turns out, paying attention is the opposite of that—it requires movement, shuffling, and transitions. Paying attention well requires focusing, unfocusing, and refocusing.

Focus is something that photographers know well. And any enthusiastic photographer will tell you that the world  looks different through the lens of a camera. Where to point the camera, which aperture to use, when to press the shutter—the decisions a photographer makes result in different images. So what might happen if you look at your own life as if through the lens of a camera? What might you notice? What might stand out? What might matter?

This experiment invites you to test the hypothesis that **using different lenses to direct your attention brings unexpected insights into focus**.

You need

A camera (it can be a smartphone)

Method

This experiment has two rounds, to be done one after the other.

Round 1

1. Find an object around you that you can move—a book, an ornament, a plant, something from your backpack or purse, a kitchen utensil, and so on.

2. With your camera, take thirty different pictures of that object. To achieve this you could move the object or change your position with respect to it. Or you may use features of the camera to change the aperture or use filters.

3. Review the pictures you took and note any insights about the object, your relationship to it, associations to other objects or concepts, or the process of getting to the thirty different images.

Round 2

4. Now jot down in your notebook a recent event or interaction with other people that you would like to understand better.

5. Inspired by your photography explorations in the first round, how many different ways can you look at that event or interaction to gain a different understanding of the situation?

6. Write down any new insights about the event or interaction that emerge from the different perspectives you try.

Reflect

▶ Use the insight-o-meter (see page 8) to gauge your insights before you move to the following page.

Assess Your Results

This experiment was inspired by the work of activist and photo facilitator Meredith Hutchison, cofounder and creative director of Resistance Communications. She gives the thirty-photographs assignment from round 1 to members of the communities she works with to produce tangible proof that every person is creative in their own right and to empower people to use art as a means of advancing the change they want to see.

In the first round of this experiment, you likely used different strategies to get to thirty different photos of your chosen object. You can think of these strategies as different sets of lenses. When you apply them to reflecting on an event or interaction, as you did in the second round, these lenses direct your attention to capture different aspects of your experience. In one of Meredith's projects, Vision Not Victim, women and girls explore their identities and career options by designing and taking photographs of their future selves in action. By directing the focus to the futures they imagine for themselves, these girls challenge stereotypes and transform how they are viewed and valued by their families and by society.

Across several experiments, Harvard University psychology professor Ellen Langer has shown that when people are instructed to change their vantage point or vary the target of their attention, they remember significantly more details about the object they had been instructed to observe compared with those who are just instructed to "pay attention." (Most people interpret that directive as "hold your focus.") For the purpose of noticing new things, adopting a soft vigilance—like a lantern that casts light softly and broadly—works better than hypervigilance—like a flashlight that projects a narrow and bright beam of light.

Here are some of the lenses you may have discovered as you conducted this experiment:

Zooming in and out. This is an extremely useful and complementary set of lenses or, more accurately, opposite extremes of an adjustable lens. In one direction, you move or zoom in closer to what you are observing to reveal details not noticeable at lower magnification. In the opposite direction, you move away or zoom out to reveal the bigger picture and explore what surrounds the object or event and how it fits into the system it's embedded in. Reflection Lab experimenter Laurie Moore said, "The up-close lens made me think about all the details of the project, which actually stressed me out a bit. But when I switched to big picture-soft focus, that lens helped me see potential outcomes, which made me relax. I also imagined what that project looked like in the grand scheme of my life, which made it feel smaller and more attainable."

Moving your vantage point. This lens requires shifting your position. You could kneel down to look from below, climb a ladder to look from above, or walk around the object. As Apollo 8 astronauts Frank Borman, James Lovell, and William Anders reached the moon on Christmas

Eve 1968, they looked back at Earth. One of the photos they took—"Earthrise (Seen for the First Time by Human Eyes)"—is among the most awe-inspiring and consequential images in human history. According to historian Robert Poole, "The sight of the whole Earth, small, alive, and alone, caused scientific and philosophical thought to shift away from the assumption that the Earth was a fixed environment, unalterably given to humankind." When reflecting on an event in this way, you may look at it from the vantage point of another participant or someone who is upstream or downstream in a collaborative process or in the hierarchy of your organization.

Not looking. Taking a photo with the camera lens covered may not make much sense for a photographer, yet it could be a most valuable lens through which to explore an experience. Barring a sight impairment, we are overly reliant on what we can see. Closing our eyes forces us to take in a situation through other senses. If you are trying to make sense of a situation, this may mean shifting your attention from someone's words to their tone of voice or the feeling you get when shaking their hand.

Turning upside-down. You may have noticed that little kids often bend down and look between their legs. This radical vantage point was embraced by art teacher Betty Edwards as a strategy to help novices learn to draw. By asking people to turn an image they were tasked with reproducing—for instance, a house or a person—upside down, they were able to see past the symbol of "house" or "person" that our brains form and notice the lines, shapes, and shadows that need to be put on paper for an accurate drawing. Similarly, if you turn a situation upside down to the point that it doesn't match the expectations that your symbolic brain has formed, you are forced to notice the actual details. One example from my experience is reframing my relationship with my students. Instead of going into a class thinking about what I will teach my students, I think about what I can learn from them. This puts me into a completely different posture—one that helps both my students and me maximize our learning.

As you reflect on past and upcoming events in your life, try on these different lenses to unlock new perspectives.

FOLLOW-UP EXPERIMENTS

Here are a few additional experiments to try, which may help you discover new lenses or tweak the ones you came up with in the first place.

Change the context. Go outside for round 1. You could just step out to your backyard, or you could travel to a very different place—a busy street, a mall, a park. You will find different kinds of objects to experiment with, which may help you uncover new lenses.

Contrast perspectives. Recruit a friend to try the experiment alongside you—using the same object for round 1 or the same event or interaction for round 2—and then compare notes.

Try tech-free waiting. The next time you find yourself waiting somewhere—for instance, at the coffee shop or in line at the grocery store—resist the urge to reach for your cell phone. Instead, look around. What do you notice that you may not have noticed before? Our cell phones help us do so many things we weren't able to do before, like staying instantly connected with friends across the globe or finding that piece of information we need in an instant. But we also use them to fill every idle moment, and, if we let them, they can get in the way of seeing what matters.

Figure Out Who You Are, Really

Your reflections are uniquely yours. They are rooted in the identities you build for yourself, the labels that society gives you, and your essence at the core. In what ways do these identities influence your actions and decisions?

Hypothesis

Daughter. Wife. Friend. Sister. Teacher. Scientist. Basketball player. Program director. Learner. I'm all of those things. But also, beneath the labels, I'm just me. Our roles and identities invite us to relate to the world and to other people in different ways. The labels that are attached to you by virtue of your formal and informal roles may change how others see you but they also affect how you see yourself. And that in turn affects how you act. Our multiple identities are complex, dynamic, and built through our relationships with others.

In this experiment, I invite you to test the hypothesis that **exploring who you are and how others see you shapes your decisions and actions**.

Method

1. In your notebook, draw two concentric circles that take up most of the page, leaving space in between them and around the outer circle (see the example on the following page).

2. In the area *outside* of the circles, jot down words or short phrases that capture elements of your identity that someone might infer or assume by looking at you or hearing your voice. Also note terms and phrases that others have used to describe you.

3. In the ring between the two circles, jot down words or phrases that describe elements of your identity that are not outwardly visible but that are known by those who really know you.

4. Now focus on the innermost circle, and jot down words or phrases that reflect elements of your identity that you keep to yourself or maybe actively hide from others.

5. Look at these circles of your identities and in your notebook, respond to the questions about your identities on the following page.

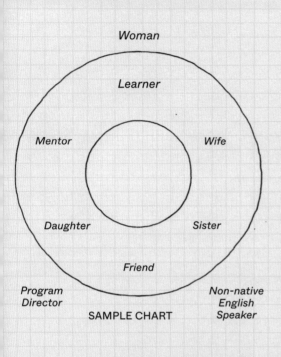

Woman

Learner

Mentor

Wife

Daughter

Sister

Friend

Program
Director

Non-native
English
Speaker

SAMPLE CHART

With which descriptors do you identify most strongly? Why is that?

With which descriptors do others identify you most strongly? How do you know? And how do you feel about that?

Describe a time when one of the elements of your identity worked to your advantage in your personal or professional life.

Describe a time when one of the elements of your identity appeared to hold you back in your personal or professional life.

6. Turn to a new page in your notebook. Now respond in writing to this question: *Who am I?* But here is the catch: you can't use any of the identities you unpacked in the previous steps or any titles or roles you may have, nor refer to anything you do (as part of your job, a hobby, or any other activity).

Reflect

▶ Use the insight-o-meter (see page 8) to gauge your insights before you move to the following page.

Assess Your Results

Reflection Lab experimenter Brigitte Lundin described this experiment as "a trip from the head to the belly." The method of this experiment draws from two sources. The first steps, which guided you to build your circles of identities, draws from the Paseo Protocol developed by educators Debbi Laidley, Debbie Bambino, Debbie McIntyre, Stevi Quate, and Juli Quinn to guide group conversations about issues of identities and values. The last part, which asked you to consider who you are in the absence of socially assigned identities, borrows from the exercise *Essence of Identity* created by facilitator Courtlandt Butts, founder of LifeGuardian Worldwide.

Reflection Lab experimenter Felipe Wilson's first reaction to his identities map was to think he was "like Dr. Jekyll and Mr. Hyde, and what people see is not who I really am." He noticed that his outside circle tended to be more positive or "light," while the inner circle reflected a more critical view of himself. The middle ring acted as "a bridge between the inside and the outside. It seems as though people who really know me

Notice

can better understand and tolerate my negative parts, and they are more flexible than me in that sense. The one word that represents this reflection for me: acceptance." **Did you notice any patterns in your circles? What word might sum up this reflection for you?**

I often find that my students may adopt what I call *limiting identities*; for example, believing that they are "not good at x," where x could be math or dancing or any other activity or discipline. This is equivalent to what psychologist and Stanford professor Carol Dweck calls having a "fixed mindset," that is, believing that you have an innate level of intelligence, creativity, or skill that can't be changed. Having a "growth mindset," on the other hand, means believing that your abilities can be developed with dedication and hard work. Another example of a limiting identity is saying "I don't participate in class because I'm an introvert." These limiting identities are problematic because they are used as excuses—to not try something new, to not engage with others. **Might any of your identities be getting in the way of your growth?**

By far the most difficult part of this experiment is the very last step: stripping away all of your labels and trying to define who you are without them. Courtlandt Butts has seen how much of a struggle this can be, especially when people identify strongly with a given title, role, or activity. In those cases, socially constructed identities can get in the way of exploring our deeper selves. Courtlandt's advice is key here: if you felt emotional while reflecting on your essential identity, it's important to name the emotions you felt, whether you felt confused, or stumped, or relieved to let go of your titles. Regardless, recognizing your moods is an essential part of the reflection process, as you explored in the first experiment of the book. **What emotions came up for you as you reflected on your essence?**

A Reflection Lab experimenter noted: "There are so many aspects of my identity that I do not share, due in part because of the societal barriers I have faced being a Black woman. The last prompt really lifted this up. I wonder how this activity might resonate with people from historically marginalized groups, particularly in the US. I could see how this could be a nice release or stir up some feelings of frustration about how many may not feel they are able to share their core self with the world."

Ashanti Branch is a civil engineer turned K–12 teacher and youth advocate. He started the nonprofit organization Ever Forward Club to help African American and Latino males reflect on the emotions they hold back and the aspects of themselves they hide behind the public image they put forth. Ashanti and his team start by inviting young people to explore two sides of themselves: qualities they gladly let people see about them "on the front of the mask" and things they usually don't let people see "on the back of the mask." **How do you feel about your ability to share your identities with others?**

The greatest value of doing this experiment can be realized by coming full circle: once you have grappled with your essential identity, go back to your circles of identities and **reflect on how that essential identity supports or comes across through your different socially constructed identities and your actions**. Take your time doing this. Go one identity at a time. Build an identity journal. This is more than an exercise to check off. It's a journey to embark on. Breathe and take the first step.

FOLLOW-UP EXPERIMENTS ◀ ◀ ◀

How have your identities changed over time? Think of yourself ten years ago (bonus points if you find a photo from that time to help you make that period of your life more vivid), repeat the experiment, and compare the results.

How does what you share on social media or on public profiles on the Web map to your circles of identities? Could your essence be distilled from what you portray? Use your map and your essential identity to do an audit of your social persona.

How do others see you? Reflection Lab experimenter Ryan Phillips asked a few friends to send him a photo of himself that they thought most represented him and then used those pictures to further reflect on his identities.

Notice

Make Sense

Reflection can reveal what's beneath the surface. This second collection of experiments helps you dig deeper to uncover what isn't obvious. Try these experiments when you are puzzling over a situation or an interaction that you'd like to make sense of.

RABBIT-HOLE.

uriosity, she ran across the fiel
as just in time to see it pop dow
hole under the hedge.

moment down went Alice after i
nsidering how in the world she
again.

ole went straight on like a tun
way, and then dipped suddenly
nly that Alice had not a momen
stopping herself before she foun
down what seemed to be a var

well was very deep, or she fe
r she had plenty of time as sh
look about her, and to wonde

Make Your Thinking Visible

Writing and sketching your thoughts and ideas are more than just ways to communicate. They are ways to make your thinking visible to yourself and others, which in turn helps you reflect on how you think.

Hypothesis

Hawaii is one of my favorite vacation destinations. I love the diversity of landscapes and activities you can explore: relaxing at the beach, horseback riding, snorkeling, hiking. Imagine you are getting ready for a Hawaiian vacation. Making a packing list can be useful. Physically placing every item from the list on top of the bed is even better. You can then get a sense of how much space each item would take, and maybe decide you can rent snorkeling gear when you get there instead of bringing your own. If you also rearrange the items into piles based on which type of activity you will use them for, you may uncover additional insights: for instance, that you included a swimsuit, hat, and sunscreen, but forgot your sandals.

Externalizing information and *thinking with your hands* as you move physical objects around is a useful exercise, even when applied to abstract concepts and ideas. If you were to enter a d.school class, it's very likely that you would encounter students working out their ideas by placing sticky notes on whiteboards. Each sticky note is an externalized thought unit—whether it's an idea or an observation. In this way it can be moved to establish connections with other thought units and to reveal patterns and breed new ideas.

In this experiment I invite you to test the hypothesis that **visualizing relationships between thoughts and ideas trains your brain to make better connections**.

Method

1. Choose one of these categories and make a list of at least ten items under that category:

Things I don't do enough

Things I want to learn

Things I am good at

Things I want to achieve this year

Ways I can make a difference

2. Jot down one item per sticky note (or cut/torn piece of paper).

3. Grab another piece of paper, turn it horizontally, and draw a line through the center, labeling the extremes "easy" and "difficult."

4. Arrange your items on this continuum. If you are using sticky notes, you can do this on a board instead.

5. Consider the map you created. Does it reveal anything you hadn't thought of before? For instance, when I did this exercise with things I want to learn, I realized there are some things that I find quite easy to learn, like removing the background of a digital image, yet I keep having to relearn them because I don't need to apply them frequently enough.

6. Replace the easy-to-difficult continuum with a few different extremes and rearrange your items accordingly. If you're using the prompt "Things I want to learn," some additional continua to try could be: I can do by myself–to–requires others; physical-to-intellectual; popular-to-unique; joyful-to-serious. Every time you finish rearranging, stop and think about whether that distribution reveals anything interesting.

Reflect

▶ Use the insight-o-meter (see page 8) to gauge your insights before you move to the following page.

Things I Want to Learn

by Reflection Lab experimenter Erica Estrada-Liou

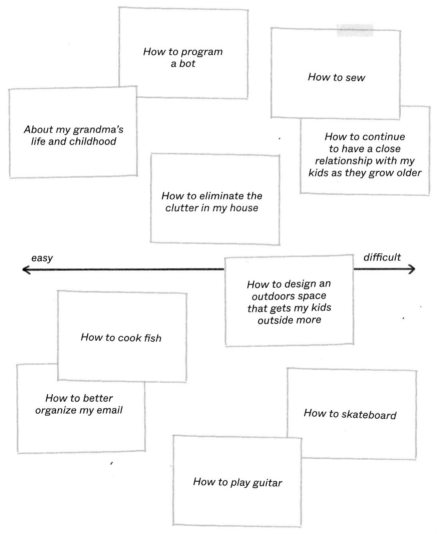

How to program a bot

How to sew

About my grandma's life and childhood

How to continue to have a close relationship with my kids as they grow older

How to eliminate the clutter in my house

easy ⟵ ⟶ difficult

How to design an outdoors space that gets my kids outside more

How to cook fish

How to better organize my email

How to skateboard

How to play guitar

✹ ✹ Assess Your Results

In this experiment you completed a sequence of three actions:

1. You created **external representations** of concepts or ideas.

2. You arranged those representations according to different **frameworks.**

3. You searched for **connections** and **patterns** in each arranged data set.

This process of externalized thinking was very useful as I was working on this book, especially in the early stages. I created an external representation of the table of contents. Each chapter got a large sticky note; concepts, stories, and people each got smaller sticky notes, all of which I constantly moved around on the wall. I rearranged the chapters to make sure the overall sequence told a story, and more than once I noticed the need to remove, replace, and add experiments.

Sticky notes have two characteristics that make them ideal physical containers for abstract thoughts: their small size forces us to narrow down concepts to their essence, and their weak but lasting adhesive allows them to be repositioned again and again. Unlike a linear list written on a piece of paper or in an electronic document, the capacity of sticky notes to be moved around in the two-dimensional space of a whiteboard or wall allows you to test out

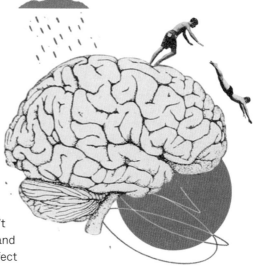

different connections between concepts, which mirrors what the reflective brain does with neurons. Some of those connections will not work. Others will click and reveal insights about the bigger issue you are exploring. Of course, you don't need sticky notes to do this, and you may achieve the same effect with simple pieces of paper.

The organizing structure you use to arrange concepts or ideas constitutes a framework. A table of contents is one example of a framework. The easy-to-difficult continuum proposed in this experiment is another. Part of the value of this exercise comes from exploring what is revealed when you tweak your frameworks. Reflection Lab experimenter Ryan Phillips organized the things he wants to learn using seven different continua, including circumstantial-to-timeless, used to designate, at one extreme, whether the usefulness of the things he wants to learn is tied to something currently happening in the world and may diminish with time or, at the other extreme, skills or knowledge that may stand the test of time.

As you rearranged the elements on your list, you may have noticed similarities and differences among the items that cluster together. You may have also realized there were items missing—things you didn't initially consider—or items that were out of place when put in the vicinity and context of other items. Noticing themes and commonalities among a group of clustered items may lead to new insights. Reflection Lab experimenter Ryan Middleton noticed that when he arranged things he doesn't do enough across the easy-to-difficult continuum, those items that clustered toward the difficult extreme all required a timely reminder, which may have been why he was not doing them. This insight pointed to a concrete action he could take. **What insights and potential actions did your externalized thinking reveal?**

FOLLOW-UP EXPERIMENTS ◀ ◀ ◀

Use a different framework. This method proposed a very simple yet powerful framework to organize information: a continuum. You can use a diversity of frameworks. One that you could try next is called "two by two" (2×2). This framework uses two continua, arranged as perpendicular axes, so you consider how the pieces of data fall into two dimensions. Using one of the prompts from the method, you could create a 2×2 with an x-axis of easy-to-difficult and a y-axis of low cost–to–high cost. In *The Secret Language of Maps*, by Carissa Carter, you'll find many more frameworks you can use as reflective tools.

Try a digital platform. Cloud-based platforms like Mural allow you to create and move around sticky notes on your computer as you would on a whiteboard or wall. For the most part you are externalizing your thinking in a way similar to the experiment proposed here. This approach lacks the process of writing by hand, which studies have shown activates parts of the brain that are not activated by typing and are beneficial for learning. On the positive side, you can more easily share, transport, and preserve your digital, externalized thought maps.

Think with others. Try externalized thinking to reflect with other people about a shared experience or to make sense of data from a joint project. As you work together in arranging the items in a data set, you may realize you are holding different assumptions about the issue at hand.

Find Questions to Your Answers

Certainty may seem like a worthy goal. Yet when you embrace what you don't know by asking lots of questions, you will be rewarded with new directions of inquiry to pursue.

Hypothesis

Keeping students safe in schools is a serious challenge. When my colleagues sam seidel and Barry Svigals from the d.school's K–12 Lab researched this topic, they did not offer solutions but instead sought to spark as many questions as possible from key stakeholders in order to illuminate the complexity of the issue. Are being safe and feeling safe the same thing? What moves the experience of learning from fear to joy? How might students be included in decision making about school safety?

Being certain feels good. Asking questions opens the door to uncertainty and may allow fear to sneak in. But doing so also catalyzes learning. Questions reveal what we don't know and challenge what we think we know for sure.

In this experiment you will test the hypothesis that **seeking questions instead of answers takes you to a new territory worth exploring**.

Sticky notes or paper and scissors
(optional: tearing the paper works too)
A timer (it can be the one in your smartphone)

Method

1. Jot down a recent event or interaction with other people that has been on your mind lately.

2. Set a timer for three to five minutes and write down as many questions as you can about that event or interaction, one question per sticky note or piece of paper, until the time is up.

3. Count the number of questions you came up with. Sort them according to the following criteria, one at a time, pausing after each round to consider what insights emerge:

- How easy it would be to get an answer, ranked from trivial to impossible

- Closed (yes/no) questions versus open-ended questions

- Questions that have one right answer versus many possible answers

- Questions that you already know the answer to versus the questions which you don't even know where to begin looking for an answer

- Questions that *you* would be able to answer versus the questions that *others* would be able to answer

4. If new questions arise as you organize and reorganize your questions, add them to the set.

5. Ask yourself these questions:

- How was the process of generating questions?
- Do you notice any patterns or a prevalent type of question among the set?
- Which of these questions most pique your curiosity?

Reflect

▶ Use the insight-o-meter (see page 8) to gauge your insights before you move to the following page.

Assess Your Results

The first thing I'd like you to notice from this experiment is that I didn't prompt you to answer the questions. How do you feel about that? It may have felt slightly uncomfortable or strange, and that's to be expected. For the most part, education rewards us for coming up with answers (and often very specific ones). Instead of finding answers, I asked you to reflect on the questions themselves and on the process of generating them.

Crafting good questions is a skill, and as such, we get better at it with practice. I hope you'll be asking yourself what constitutes a good question. Here is one simple answer: A good question is one that makes you more curious—one that nudges you into a state of not knowing so that you may consider new possibilities. You can ask good questions that do this for others, and, importantly, you can do this for yourself too. The latter was the goal of this experiment, but I invite you to try the former too.

Certain types of questions are more likely to achieve this effect of amplifying your curiosity.

Why . . . ? *Why* questions are an authentic manifestation of curiosity—one that children seem to never get tired of asking and that adults should ask more often. Asking *why* is one way to probe beneath what's visible or evident. Asking why multiple times helps you dig deeper to unearth what's at the root of an issue.

What if . . . ? *What if* questions invite us to consider possibilities. What is being asked is framed as a hypothesis and implies that we are temporarily suspending judgment and disbelief. This can work in conversation with others to create a space where it feels safe to propose ideas or scenarios that could be considered far-fetched. It is equally powerful to use that same *what if* framing to get past our own internal censor—the voice that is quick to tell us our bold ideas will never work. Another use of *what if* questions is to speculate about counterfactual scenarios at the personal level—*What if I had accepted that job?*—or beyond—*What if all humans had access to clean water?*

How might I/we . . . ? A *how might I/we* question is a powerful way to frame a challenge for which we seek novel solutions. The *how* invites thinking about concrete ways to achieve the goal that is the focus of the question. The *might*—as opposed to *will*—recognizes that success is uncertain, which is a good target in innovative work for which there are no guaranteed outcomes. If we are using the *we* version of this question, this implies a collective effort. And here is one important related question to ask: *Who* are *we*? Are you including a diversity of perspectives in your work and process? Can you codesign with people who have a lived experience related to the challenge or opportunity you are tackling? A great modifier to add to *how might I/we* questions is *else*. Asking "How *else* might I/we . . ." invites us to find multiple and alternative ways to achieve something and prevents us from narrowing down our options too soon.

FOLLOW-UP EXPERIMENT

Try question-storming. How many questions did you come up with for the experiment? Can you craft ten more? Twenty more? **Can you push yourself to get to a hundred questions?** Add a five-minute question-storming at the beginning of each day or right before a meeting. How does that change how you approach your day or your stance during the meeting? One reason we might avoid asking questions is the perception that it makes us look less trustworthy. Karen Huang and her colleagues at Harvard University have found the opposite to be true: Asking questions makes others like you more. Bank on this finding and **practice asking more questions in your interactions with others**. It is a great way to learn from different perspectives.

Climb the Ladder of Meaning

When you get stuck trying to solve a problem, coming up with new and loftier problems can lift you up over the hurdles. You may discover you were moving down a narrow path that wouldn't take you where you want to go.

Hypothesis

Bernie Roth, a d.school founder and engineering professor, will tell you that if you have a problem you can't solve, you are most likely trying to solve the wrong problem. In his book, *The Achievement Habit*, Bernie shares many strategies from his personal life that have helped his students get unstuck and realize their potential. One of those strategies is to change the question you are trying to answer. By moving between the concrete and the abstract, you can discover which problems are a better fit for where you are and what you want to achieve. This is a key ability of designers. For example, trying to solve food insecurity is a commendable goal, but the question of how to do so may be too abstract. Where would you even start? Aiming to provide nutritious meals to families in need in your neighborhood may be a more concrete and achievable goal. But there could be other approaches worth considering, too, like rewriting policies that contribute to the food insecurity of those families in the first place.

In this experiment I invite you to test the hypothesis that **exploring multiple levels of abstraction helps you discover what really matters and better ways to get there**.

Method

Read through the instructions, then check out the sample diagram on the following page before you start working.

1. Starting at the bottom of a blank page, jot down a current goal you have.

2. Draw an arrow going up from that goal and complete the prompt, "This could allow me to . . ."

3. Continue to answer the same prompt for each new statement you write, moving *up* the page. When you get to a statement that feels too abstract, it's time to stop (see my example for an illustration of this).

4. Now draw an arrow from the side of your initial goal and complete the prompt, "I could do this by . . ." Come up with at least three different solutions.

5. Repeat step 4 for the other derivative goals in your ladder. Always come up with at least three alternatives for each goal.

6. Finally, evaluate the whole set of goals and possible solutions you drafted. Do you see a goal that may be a better fit than the one you started with? A solution that you hadn't considered before? Write down any ideas and insights that emerged from the process.

Reflect

▶ Use the insight-o-meter (see page 8) to gauge your insights before you move to the following page.

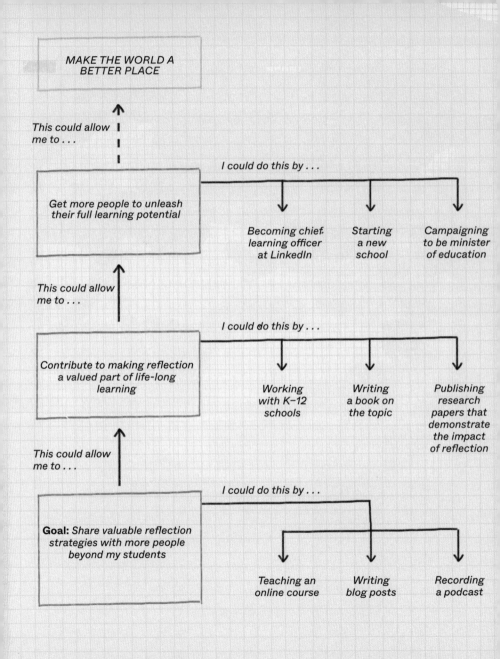

Assess Your Results

This method is an adaptation of a "ladder of abstraction" or "why-how ladder," which originates in the work of linguist S. I. Hayakawa. This adaptation activates two types of thinking that expand our abilities to make sense of the world: imagination and divergent thinking.

By asking you to complete the prompt "This could allow me to . . ." for a goal you have, I invited you to explore deeper, implicit motivations behind that goal—in other words, your whys. In some cases those motivations may have been clear to you at the outset, yet in doing this exercise you may have also discovered other potential motives to pursue that goal. Your starting point for the exercise could be a personal goal, as my example was, or it could be a strategy being deployed by a company or a new product going out to the market.

Going up the ladder took you from what *is* to what *could be.* By entertaining what could be possible—even those options that sound improbable—you are engaging your imagination and pushing yourself outside of the familiar. As you go up the ladder, goals tend to be more abstract. If you keep moving in that direction, you will eventually arrive at some version of "to make the world a better place"—a lofty goal, yes, but way too general to be useful.

Going in the other direction, your answers to "I could do this by . . ." move you toward concrete solutions and actions— the hows—down the ladder of abstraction. I asked you to

come up with at least three different solutions. In doing so you engaged in divergent thinking. Have you ever fallen into the trap of moving ahead with the first idea that comes to mind? Chances are this idea is not the best one. By pausing to think about how *else* you could achieve something, you open the range of possibilities and give yourself more options to choose from. **How easy was it to come up with those alternatives?** It's normal to struggle to generate new ideas, but it becomes easier with practice.

Since you can go up and down from any rung of the ladder, you might end up with a structure that resembles a jungle gym—a lattice more than a ladder. The value of this exercise is in the process of exploring the problem in all directions and expanding the realm of possibilities as a means to reflect on what really matters to you. On his website, the computer scientist and mathematician Don Knuth explains that he hasn't had an email address in decades, so he can stay focused on writing his computer science textbook: "Email is a wonderful thing for people whose role in life is to be on top of things. But not for me; my role is to be on the bottom of things." As you move up and down the lattice you created, **what position feels more promising and more likely to propel you toward your goals?**

FOLLOW-UP EXPERIMENT

Exercise your divergent thinking muscles with constraints. Consider a problem you have and generate a list of two or three possible solutions. Start with the obvious ones. Then push yourself to get to ten or twenty alternative solutions for the same problem. If you feel stuck, try coming up with a few solutions that conform to any of the following categories:

Involving an unlikely collaborator

Inspired by a brand you like

Evoking the feeling of summer camp

Incorporating music or sound

Constraints such as these categories help the process of generating more diverse ideas because they give you boundaries and a concrete starting point instead of a wide-open space that may be intimidating. As you work on coming up with multiple alternatives, consider that even those ideas that seem fanciful, impractical, or out of reach may inspire new, more achievable and practical ideas you hadn't thought of before.

Travel through the Wormholes of Reflection

Language is more than a way to communicate. It is also a tool to think. Using words that evoke images can help you make unexpected connections and find new meanings in your experiences.

Hypothesis

Physicists use the term *wormhole* to describe a hypothetical tunnel that connects different points in space, time, or even different universes. When we speak or write, metaphors act as wormholes, helping us connect an abstract concept with something more concrete and familiar. *Don't keep me in the dark. I'm drowning in paperwork.* These are common sayings that show the utility of metaphors. It's likely that, as you read those two examples, your mind conjured an image that conveyed the meaning.

We can use metaphors in reflection to spark instant connections that help us discover new dimensions in our experiences. When we think about important moments in our lives, we may get stuck in the universe of meaning that is closer to that moment or more familiar to us. For instance, when I was working on this book, as I moved around the house or took a quick trip to the supermarket, everything I noticed seemed to be related to the content of the book. This was useful for my writing process, but I may have also missed the opportunity to notice and make connections to other areas of my life and work. I was temporarily stuck in a universe of meaning revolving around the book. Using metaphors allows us to intentionally escape from the universes of meaning that are top of mind or habitual.

This experiment invites you to test the hypothesis that **creating metaphors transports you to different universes of meaning.**

Method

1. Think back on your previous week and complete the following sentences in your notebook. If these prompts don't elicit anything about your week, just list one to three moments that are top of mind.

   • A moment I felt challenged was when . . .

   • A moment I hesitated was when . . .

   • A moment I felt accomplished was when . . .

2. To build your metaphor generator, organize sixteen strips of paper into two piles of eight. On the paper strips in one pile, write down the following adjectives, one word per strip: Gentle, Funny, Burning, Desperate, Unpredictable, Elusive, Silent, Loud. Fold the strips in half to conceal the adjective. On the other pile of paper strips, write down the following nouns, one word per strip: Mirror, Lens, Trophy, Melody, Adventure, Animal, Disguise, Miracle. Again fold the strips in half. Shuffle each pile, keeping the piles separate. This is your metaphor generator, and it is ready to run!

3. Unfold one piece of paper from each pile and place them side by side to form an adjective + noun combination. Go through the list of moments you captured and consider how the combination you drew might connect with each moment on your list. Use the following prompts:

     How is [moment 1] like a(n) [adjective + noun combo you drew]?

     What would follow from that?

4. Jot down anything that comes to mind in response, even if it doesn't make perfect sense at first.

Repeat!

Do any of the connections bring up something about your moments that you hadn't thought of before? If so, elaborate on it by freewriting in your notebook.

Reflect

▶ Use the insight-o-meter (see page 8) to gauge your insights before you move to the following page.

Assess Your Results

You may be familiar with connect-the-dots puzzles, in which drawing lines that connect numbered points on a page reveals an image. As it turns out, that's what our brains do to learn and make sense of the world, with neurons instead of dots. Concepts and memories are encoded in the brain in networks of neurons that fire up when we direct our attention to that concept or memory. By turning your attention simultaneously to a personal experience and the image elicited by the combination of words (adjective + noun in this case), you are in essence forcing the connection between separate networks of neurons. Some of those connections—but not all—may reveal a useful insight. When that happens, you have in effect created a new network that encodes new information you can use moving forward.

After running this exercise, Reflection Lab experimenter Erica Estrada-Liou reflected: "A metaphor I drew from the generator helped me arrive at an insight that wasn't new to the world per se, but it was new to me. As a result, I changed my mind about an action I intended to take. Looking back at my reflection, I started having new questions. Reflections breed more questions than answers, and that's valuable!"

Reflection Lab experimenter Ilya Avdeev said: "I noticed a correlation between the number of new thoughts the metaphors brought up and how emotionally charged my selected moment was. The first moment (something

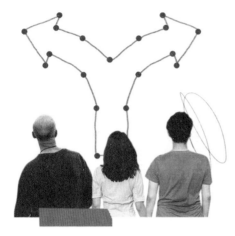

challenging) had been occupying my mind for several days, and the metaphors created new ways of thinking about it. I also had to 'park' a few metaphors that led to nothing new (like 'stingy mirror' or 'silent animal'). The three new reflections that came up in the next round were quite different. Perhaps the first round served as therapy and allowed me to kick the first moment out of my mind and focus on other moments."

Some words from the metaphor generator were unfamiliar to some experimenters in the Reflection Lab. If that was the case for you, you can always replace them or add new words. It's your generator, so feel free to customize it.

Some experimenters set a timer for two to three minutes for each word combination to keep a constant pace and move through the experiment; others found that being patient and persevering with combinations that initially didn't seem to elicit any connections eventually paid off. What rhythm worked for you?

FOLLOW-UP EXPERIMENTS

Metaphor generator v2. Instead of adjective + noun, build a metaphor generator with adverb + verb, such as: Cautiously, Gently, Thankfully, Blindly, Patiently, Wildly, Mysteriously, Lovingly + Dance, Grow, Laugh, Eat, Drive, Dive, Observe, Question.

Time travel. Try the metaphor generator with anticipated future moments as a means to get ready for those moments. (For more on reflecting forward, see Experiment #9. The metaphor generator is a good tool to use—again—after Experiment #9.)

INSPIRATION

REFLECTION 7

ABBEY

Envision

Reflection and imagination are not at odds. In fact, they can reinforce each other toward building better futures for yourself and others. Tap into this third collection of experiments when you need to stretch your time horizons, escape the hamster wheel of short-term thinking, and find inspiration to move forward with your personal and professional adventures.

!1&&e.stopOnFalse
th:r&&(s=t,c(r))}
return u=[],this},disable:
ction(){return p.fireWith(this,argu
,r={state:function(){return n},alw
e.promise().done(n.resolve).fail
on(){n=s},t[1^e][2].disable,t[2
(arguments),r=n.length,i=1!==
(r);r>t;t++)n[t]&&b.isFunctio
")[0],r.style.cssText="to
readystatechange",H),e.at
ing Function Array Date
e){var t=_[e]={};return
OnFalse){r=!1;break}n=
c(r))}return this},r
this},disable:funct
.fireWith(this,arg
on(){return n},al
(n.resolve).fail
[2].disable,t[2
length,i=1!==
&b.isFunctio
>a</a><inpu

Reflect
Forward

You may not think of yourself as a futurist,
but you are shaping what's to come with every
action you take. By activating your capacity to
reflect *forward*, you can engage in the unscripted
adventure of life with intention and boldness.

Hypothesis

We tend to associate reflection with looking back. It's only natural. We spend years in school studying history. Yet, in a world full of uncertainty and complex challenges, education should prepare us not only to be knowledgeable about the past but also give us the skills to build the future. That is what "futures literacy" is about.

MIT professor and philosopher Donald Schön proposed two reflection modes: *reflection-on-action* (reflecting after the experience) and *reflection-in-action* (reflecting during the experience). This experiment is about uncovering the power of a third type of reflection: *reflection-for-action*, which I call *proflection,* as it is about projecting ourselves into the future.

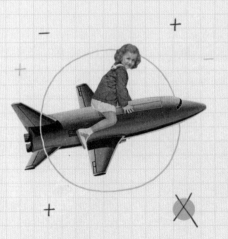

Futurist and design strategist Lisa Kay Solomon brought the rich methods and mindsets of futures thinking to the d.school as a designer in residence. Borrowing from the toolkit she introduced to us, this experiment invites you to test the hypothesis that **imagining a multitude of possible futures allows you to steer toward the one you aspire to create.**

Method

1. Think about your everyday life or work. What is something that is a central part of it? It could be a product or tool that you use all the time, the space where you work, or incentives that are valued by you or others. Come up with a few candidates. Then, in your notebook, draw a circle at the center of a blank page and write "A world without X" inside the circle, where X is one of the elements you identified. For instance, as an educator I may write, "A world without classrooms" (other possible Xs on my list: grades, textbooks, exams, diplomas, selective admissions, disciplines, and so on).

2. Imagine the consequences of removing that element. To make it easier, start thinking about the coming week. What might happen in a world in which X doesn't exist? Write all the consequences down, drawing arrows from the central circle. Consider both positive and negative consequences, and code them as such with a plus or minus sign. If you can't quite categorize some as either positive or negative, add them anyway.

3. Now extend your thinking further. Starting from each of the first-order consequences you imagined, add second-order consequences, both positive and negative. Can you go even further and think of third-order consequences?

Envision

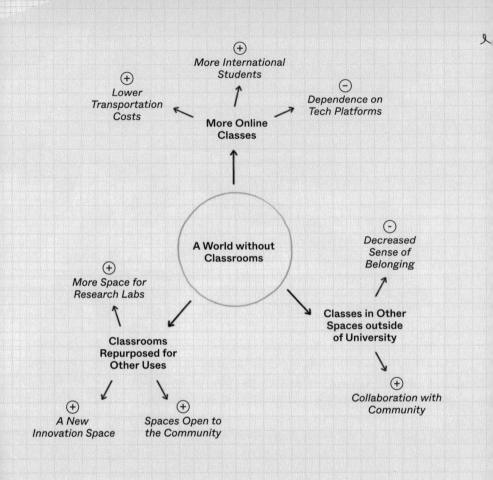

Reflect

▶ Use the insight-o-meter (see page 8) to gauge your insights before you move to the following page.

Assess Your Results

This experiment adapts a method for exploring consequences called the Futures Wheel, invented by Jerome C. Glenn in 1971. You may have noticed that it's "futures," not the singular "future." That's an important detail. As I suggested in the introduction, there is no such thing as *the* future. There are many possible paths ahead of us. You made that evident with the wheel you crafted. You can follow any number of paths from the center of the wheel, and each will paint a distinct possible future.

Think of the starting point. When it comes to prospecting possible futures, the present can get in the way. That's why I invited you to start by removing an element that you see as important in your life or work. By doing this you create a gap that your imagination can fill with alternatives. This first step alone can be challenging, and it takes practice. As creatures of habit, we get used to tools and routines and start thinking of them as indispensable. When new alternatives emerge, people may experience varying degrees of resistance. Fast forward a few (or many) years and we tend to habituate to the alternative, often forgetting that what was replaced existed in the first place. When it comes to determining the starting point for your wheel, just the thought of getting rid of elements you think are essential may make you feel uncomfortable or skeptical. If you can work through those emotions and suspend your disbelief, removing those things will probably yield the most provocative results.

Weave imagined futures.
As you connect the potential consequences you mapped, you can weave many possible paths that may include negative and positive events. This is what *reflection-for-action* or *proflection* is about. The futures wheel is not a planning tool but a prospecting tool; your goal is to consider as many consequences as possible, and it's crucial to be both optimistic and pessimistic. **The goal of forward reflection is not to impose your will on the future but to embrace uncertainty and open yourself to possibilities.** It is natural to avoid considering potential negative outcomes, whether consciously or unconsciously. Yet including them is essential. If we engage in proflection and map as many unintended consequences as we can imagine, we can also come up with ways to prevent them.

Act now. As you consider this multiplicity of futures, what do you find exciting? And what actions could you take today to drive toward those futures? On the flip side, what are the future possibilities that concern or even terrify you? And what actions could you take (or refrain from taking) today to steer clear of those futures? By asking yourself these questions, you increase your agency over your destiny.

FOLLOW-UP EXPERIMENTS

Start with hope. Think of an outcome you wish would happen within the coming months or years and place it at the center. Then imagine that this outcome has come to pass and build a futures wheel starting from that premise.

Reflect forward with others. The futures you imagine collaboratively with people who bring different lived experiences and domain expertise will be different from those you come up with on your own.

Build Futures You Can Touch

The objects we use every day say a lot about how we spend our time and what interests us. Imagining future versions of these objects makes possible futures concrete, which in turn makes it possible to reflect on those futures.

Hypothesis

Artifacts are physical or digital objects made by human beings. Imagine for a moment that the space where you are right now, and all the artifacts in it, freeze in time and become an exhibit in a museum a hundred years into the future. Through the artifacts displayed, the visitors to that exhibit will get a glimpse into your world and into the broader society in which those artifacts were created. If my current scene was the exhibit, people may gather that a portable computer seems to be central to many of my daily activities. They may puzzle at the words scribbled on sticky notes that are arranged in clusters on the wall, and if they examined the active playlist on my phone, they would get a sense of the music I like to listen to.

Now let's step out of that imaginary museum but stay in that future—a hundred years from today. Picture yourself as an inhabitant of that future, going about the activities in your daily routines. What artifacts may exist in a hundred years to facilitate these activities and even help you do things that you can't do today? This experiment invites you to test the hypothesis that **reimagining everyday objects activates your ability to conceive possible futures.**

Method

1. Imagine yourself doing either an everyday activity— like eating dinner, exercising at the gym, receiving a package, or calling a friend—or attending a special event like a wedding, a vacation, or a conference. Where are you? What do you see around you? In your notebook, list the objects you see. For instance, if I were at the supermarket shopping for groceries I might see shopping carts, baskets, shelves with lots of different products, a cash register, refrigerators, and posters advertising products and discounts.

2. Choose one of the objects you see and imagine how it might be different in a future that excites you. What new features and capabilities might this object have that would allow you to do new things in this setting? Do this by sketching or building a version of that object with your materials. Label any new features. This doesn't have to be an artistic sketch or a realistic construction. Use lines, shapes, and simple materials to think with your hands.

Reflect

▶ Use the insight-o-meter (see page 8) to gauge your insights before you move to the following page.

✹ ✹ Assess Your Results

How easy or difficult was it for you to come up with a list of objects that you interact with in everyday activities? As we get used to our routines, the objects that make them possible may fade into the background of our awareness. Noticing this shift in your awareness is an excellent first step. Make a point of observing objects during your next activity of the day, or simply stop reading right now and look around you. **Which artifacts do you see?**

When Reflection Lab experimenter Joseph Samosky ran this experiment, he placed himself and his wife in their garden tending the vegetables. It's fall harvest time, and they are surrounded by tomatoes: bright orange Sungolds, yellow Nebraska Weddings, and pink-red Pink Brandywines. They have armfuls of organic veggies and want to take a selfie with their colorful bounty to send to their family. This turns out to be hard to do, since they are juggling delicate, very ripe tomatoes and trying to get both of them in the frame at the same time. So Joseph takes his iPhone 27, which he has imagined with a built-in "levitation tripod ability," holds the camera at arm's length, and then gives it a gentle push so it floats back a couple of feet and stabilizes in midair. It takes a few holograms and sends them to the family.

How was the process of sketching or building your artifact from the future? Did you have a fully formed idea before you started sketching or building? If you didn't, that's exactly right. Part of the value of this exercise is to practice building as a way to think (sketching is building in two dimensions) and letting ideas emerge in the process. Joseph used his real phone and a plastic bag as he thought through his "dirigible self-positioning floating iPhone."

Whether an artifact like the one you crafted will exist in the future is not the most interesting question to ask. Rather, what questions about the present are sparked by the artifact you created? When Joseph shared his idea with a teaching assistant, the assistant mentioned having seen videos of people who have had accidents while attempting to take a selfie. This opened a new dimension related to the potential of enhanced safety. They also discussed how many of us may ask a passerby to take a picture when it's hard to fit everyone in a selfie. Joseph recalled having recently approached two people to take a photo of him and his wife after finishing a 5K run. They struck up an interesting conversation that would not have happened if they had owned a levitating selfie camera. So he discovered a negative social implication to the new camera he imagined.

If you stroll past the front window at 201 Hamilton Street in Palo Alto, California, as I've done often, you may see some interesting products on display. Looking for a smart voice assistant for your home? You could consider a "Sustainabot." It will not only dim your lights when you ask, but it can also "coach your family to lead a greener lifestyle." Here's the thing, though. Not only is Sustainabot not for sale, it doesn't even exist. This "store" front belongs to the Institute for the Future. Creating artifacts from the future is one of the

institute's strategies to spark conversations about possible futures—both intended and unintended. When envisioning how we might work or live many years from now, artifacts make those futures tangible.

You can also use artifacts as a strategy to inspire others to see a change you want to create in a more immediate future. This is what designers call prototyping. When University Innovation Fellow and engineering student Alexandra Seda set out to collaborate with Ohio Northern University staff in envisioning a library that would engage a new generation of students, she procured as many discarded large cardboard boxes as she could get and took them to the library. Along with Adam Berry and other students, she built different life-size cardboard furniture pieces. Interacting with and moving the cardboard artifacts around helped the team envision and explore what would work for the new library before spending any resources.

Whether you want to project yourself toward a remote future or you need to convey your vision for a more immediate future, **crafting tangible artifacts stimulates the senses, generates ideas, and invites conversations**.

FOLLOW-UP EXPERIMENTS

Try any of these variations of this experiment:

Instead of thinking of a future you want to see, create an artifact from a future that terrifies you.

Instead of building an artifact, role-play an experience from the future.

Show your artifact to someone else and use it as a conversation starter about the future.

Don't Finish
What You
Sta . . .

Your calendar, your to-do lists, the milestones set
by the organization you work for—they all reveal
and shape your priorities. Reflecting on the time
horizons you are setting your sights on can help
you reassess what is worth doing.

Hypothesis

The field of prospective psychology proposes that the ability to think about (prospect) the future is uniquely human. In his thought-provoking book *The Good Ancestor*, philosopher Roman Krznaric highlights the moment when, twelve thousand years ago, our ancestors started saving seeds to plant; he calls this "the symbolic birth of long-term thinking." Accordingly, he coined the term *acorn brain* to describe our prospecting abilities. However, most people do not make plans beyond fifteen to twenty years, and the anticipation of our death seems to be a mental barrier. Prospecting the future beyond our lifetimes takes practice.

In this experiment, I invite you to test the hypothesis that **thinking about what you could start instead of what you need to finish helps you plant seeds for a better future for the generations to come.**

Method

1. Think about something you are working on that's due within the **next five days** or so. In your notebook, write down a headline for the project and answer the following questions: *Why am I doing it? And, if I am successful, who will benefit?*

2. Then think about something you want to achieve in the **next five years**. As before, write down a headline for the project and answer the same questions: *Why am I doing it? And, if I am successful, who will benefit?*

3. Finally, think about a project that you could start but that would take **at least a hundred years** to complete. Do the same as you did for the other two projects, but this time answer one more question: *Who could take over and continue this project?*

Reflect

▶ Use the insight-o-meter (see page 8) to gauge your insights before you move to the following page.

✳ ✳ Assess Your Results

As you consider the three projects you outlined, **how does your sense of urgency change?** I don't know about you, but when I think about what I need to get done this week, I get anxious. It feels like the number of overdue items on my to-do list grows by the minute. Preoccupied with the urgent, we don't always have time for the important. And it's not only our calendars that cause stress. It's the news cycle in which what happens today seamlessly replaces what happened yesterday in our consciousness. It's the politicians who think in terms of what's going to get them a win in the next election. It's the companies chasing after quarterly revenues. At the other extreme, we are faced with complex problems, like climate change and environmental degradation, for which there is no immediate solution, and it feels overwhelming to even think about where to start to tackle them. So we push them to the back of our mind.

How did you fare in coming up with your hundred-year project? Have you ever considered such a timeline? You may be thinking, *Why even start a project that I can't possibly finish? Who will take it over?* That's exactly why you should start such a project—because you can't finish it, and it requires the participation of future generations. It is an invitation to reframe your role as part of a continuum of humans that can and should collaborate across generations toward building a better world.

In his essay "The Big Here and Long Now," musician and visionary Brian Eno urges us to change our relationship with time. He asks, "Can we become inspired by the prospect of contributing to the future? Can we extend our empathy to the lives beyond ours?" The hundred-year project I invited you to draft is but a blink compared with the Clock of the Long Now, a massive mechanical structure designed to tick for ten thousand years. Conceived by Danny Hillis of the Long Now Foundation (of which Eno is also a member), the clock is currently being built inside a mountain in Texas. This and other similar art projects aim to inspire us to broaden our time horizons and reconsider the decisions we make in the present.

When we introduce students to design at the d.school, we make sure that they grapple with the multiple dimensions that may be affected—both positively and negatively—by what they create and put out into the world. These dimensions span different scales of time. Products and services, both physical and digital, may come and go at a fast pace, driven by market forces and the whims of fashion and trends. But the ripple effects those products can initiate may affect society, and even nature, in consequential ways that are not always immediately apparent.

With his Pace Layers model, Stewart Brand, cochair and president of the Long Now Foundation, proposes a way to stretch our thinking about time and how our contributions fit into the evolution of civilization. According to Brand's model, a healthy system can be understood in terms of six layers, each operating at its own pace: Fashion/Art, Economics, Infrastructure, Governance, Culture, and Nature. The top layer of Fashion/Art moves quickly—in days and months—and is the most likely to grab our attention. This is where we find the latest TikTok dance challenges and gender reveal parties, as well as ridesharing and plant-based meat alternatives. The next layer, Economics, sifts through the rapid flow of new products and ideas to salvage what makes commercial sense. One layer down, Infrastructure provides the foundations for society to operate—in the form of transportation, energy, communications, education, and science, which require investments that are longer term than what commerce can support. The following two layers, Governance and Culture, are even slower to change, preserving lasting values and spanning multiple facets of our lives. Finally, Nature is the slowest changing layer and also the most powerful. In a healthy system, the different layers communicate and provide feedback to one another while moving at their own speed.

As you consider the three projects you outlined with respect to these layers moving at different speeds, answer the following questions:

What layers might you have overlooked with your one-week and five-year projects? While most immediate outcomes from those projects may fall in the fast-moving layers, even small, short-term actions eventually affect slower moving layers of civilization when a large number of people engage in them.

How do you envision your hundred-year project affecting the slow-moving layers of Culture and Nature? Think of the change you aspire to create, but also the dangers you want to avoid.

What metrics are appropriate to assess success in each of your three projects? As you adapt to long-term thinking, consider whether you may be prematurely judging something as a failure before it's reasonable to expect an outcome. You won't get to see the end of your hundred-year project, by design. **What might be some milestones indicating you are steering it toward a productive initial trajectory?**

Finishing projects is overvalued. Ask yourself instead: **What is a project that is worth starting despite not being able to finish it?**

FOLLOW-UP EXPERIMENTS ◀ ◀ ◀

Nudge your acorn brain. Establish a practice of writing dates with a five-digit year (for example, this book was published in the year 02023). According to the Long Now Foundation, adding the leading zero may tickle your sense of time and offer perspective every time you write the date.

Collaborate across generations. Invite a young person to design a long-term project that you could collaborate on. What new perspectives and considerations might they bring to the project?

Be a Good Ancestor

Your present life is connected to the lives of both past and future generations. Reflection can help make these links visible, and this in turn can shape how you understand the consequences of your decisions and actions.

Hypothesis

Kelsey Juliana was nineteen years old when she—along with twenty other young people, one as young as eight—sued the US government. In *Juliana v. United States*, the plaintiffs claim that the government continues to allow the exploitation of fossil fuels despite knowing that this practice has a catastrophic and irreversible impact on the environment. By doing so they disproportionately affect young people and unborn future generations, who are on track to inherit a degraded environment that won't support their rights to life, liberty, and property. In the words of the polio vaccine inventor Jonas Salk, "Are we being good ancestors?" Sadly, the evidence says we are not.

In this experiment I invite you to cultivate the long-term thinking that is needed to become a good ancestor. The hypothesis to test is that **connecting with the inhabitants of the future helps you think differently about your decisions and contribute to intergenerational justice**.

Method

1. Imagine someone you know and care about from a previous generation. It could be a parent or grandparent. Imagine them as a young adult and ask yourself the following questions. You don't need to *know* the answers; it's okay to imagine what they might be.

   - What did my ancestor see and feel when they woke up every morning?

   - What gave my ancestor a sense of purpose at that age?

   - What brought my ancestor joy? Who did they surround themself with?

   - What vision(s) did my ancestor have for the future? What did they want for me?

2. Breathe in and out slowly as you come back to your present. Pause.

3. Now think of a young person in your life with whom you feel connected. It could be a niece, a child of your own, or the child of friends. Bring to mind their face and voice and imagine them doing what they love.

4. Imagine you have traveled twenty years into the future. What is going on with them now? What are they doing? What do they care about? What does the world around them look like?

5. Move further into the future and imagine the following scene: It's this same person's eightieth birthday celebration, and they are surrounded by their friends, family, and colleagues. They see a photo of you on the wall and they are reminded of fond memories and the legacy you left them. They turn to their children and grandchildren and tell them what they learned from you, what you did that positively affected them, and how you inspired them. In your notebook, write down what they say.

Reflect

▶ Use the insight-o-meter (see page 8) to gauge your insights before you move to the following page.

Assess Your Results

How did it *feel* to imagine the legacy you will leave to future generations? In *The Good Ancestor*, philosopher Roman Krznaric claims that becoming a good ancestor is a formidable task, one that requires us to shift the time-scale of our thinking. Our short-term myopia prevents us from seeing the impact of our actions beyond our lifetime.

My d.school colleague Louie Montoya has facilitated an activity similar to the one outlined in this method, and he finds that it often stirs discomfort among the group. He says, "I just give people permission to feel weird about this activity. For some it might be fun but for others it might be painful." It takes courage and patience to sit with those emotions. Using the emotions that come up for you to reflect on your present choices and actions can be transformative. **Are your current behaviors and beliefs in line with your ability to be a good ancestor? What changes can you make today? What actions can you commit to?**

The case for a legacy mindset and the need for intergenerational justice could be made on the basis of numbers alone: if we look fifty thousand years into the past and fifty thousand years into the future, the nearly seven trillion unborn humans to come far outweigh the hundred billion who have lived on Earth to date. Yet it is hard to feel empathy for a group of anonymous future humans, however large that group may be.

The goal of this exercise, adapted from an activity devised by the Long Time Project cofounders Bea Karol Burks and Ella Saltmarshe, is to create a personal connection with the inhabitants of the future and think in concrete terms about the legacy we are leaving them.

For Reflection Lab experimenter Jessica Aldrich, this exercise was a reminder that "there are many who came before me who had thoughts, feelings, and experiences that I can't begin to know or understand. But they were whole people with whole lives before I came into the picture." She goes on, "A legacy is more than just an idea of what we want to be known for; it's a continuation of the lives that came before us and poured into us and how we use that to influence the lives that will come after us." This logic has been ingrained in principles and practices of indigenous peoples worldwide for a long time. One example is the seventh-generation principle of the Iroquois Nations, which urges those in the current generation to make decisions and act for the benefit of the seventh generation that will come after them.

As *Juliana v. United States* pursues its meandering path through the slow-moving US justice system, there are actions we can take as individuals to make sure that we center the interests of the future generations in our projects and decisions.

FOLLOW-UP EXPERIMENTS ◀ ◀ ◀

Invite young people to participate in activities you organize. This could be presentations, codesign sessions, conferences, and more. Assign them an active role, not one that is merely symbolic. For the past few years, I've invited middle school students to come to my class and coach university students on idea generation. Not only do these young people model for their older peers the power of an active imagination, but they also bring their own perspectives to the design challenges we are tackling.

The empty chair technique. This is used by therapists to help patients practice talking to a specific person. As a variation, try leaving an empty chair at your meetings to represent a person from a future generation and to remind yourself and those you work with of the interests and rights of these future-holders who would otherwise be invisible.

Name future generations in the reports and documents you produce and in your mission statements. Take inspiration from the more than forty national constitutions that have been amended in the last few decades to explicitly mention the rights of future generations.

Reflecting on Reflection and Becoming a Reflective Practitioner

If you have ever played competitive sports or exercised at the gym, you probably recognize the value of having a coach to suggest an exercise, motivate you to keep going, or nudge you to challenge yourself a bit more. I designed this book to provide some of that same value by offering you methods to explore different facets of reflection, stories to inspire and motivate you, and self-assessments that invite you to push yourself to grow.

Like physical exercise, reflection works best when it's built into your daily routine rather than something you do every now and then. As with any habit, you must be intentional about incorporating reflection in a way that sticks and that you can maintain. Here are some ways to become a reflective practitioner.

Build a Pensieve

Reflection scholar Jenny Moon proposes the pensieve, a device from Harry Potter's fictional world, as a useful metaphor to grasp the meaning and value of reflection.

In *Harry Potter and the Goblet of Fire*, the wizard Albus Dumbledore describes how to use the pensieve: "One simply siphons the excess thoughts from one's mind, pours them into the basin, and examines them at one's leisure. It becomes easier to spot patterns and links, you understand, when they are in this form."

A pensieve is, in essence, a container for reflection. Dumbledore's pensieve had the appearance of a metal basin. Your container will look entirely different. Let's explore building blocks you can use to design your own pensieve: moment, medium, sharing, and prompts.

Moment

Experimenting with the timing and frequency of reflection is key. You could choose to reflect every day or once a week; in the morning or the evening; or at specific moments, for instance in preparation for a weekly team check-in. Those who study the formation of habits recognize the power of choosing the right moment. If you add reflection immediately following an action you already perform regularly, this will go a long way in establishing a *habit* of reflection. The action could be turning on your computer in the morning or preparing a cup of tea at the end of the day.

Consider also how reflection may contribute to specific projects. In this case, reflection should not be relegated to the tail end. Reflecting at the outset of a project or in preparation for a meeting or conversation—what I call *preflection*—is equally if not more valuable. The methods in the third collection of experiments are particularly useful for this.

Medium

You may go physical or digital here; each has advantages. The physical options range from a notebook to sticky notes that you place on your computer monitor or the fridge. Software evolves too fast to mention any specific program, but you could opt to use the simple notepad app that comes with your smartphone or go with a more sophisticated program that allows you to systematically organize, search, annotate, and highlight your notes.

I encourage you to also experiment with a medium that allows you to sketch and insert images.

Sharing

Sharing is not just a way to communicate your thoughts; it can also affect how you reflect. When you share your reflections with people who have different perspectives and levels of understanding, you must make decisions about what's important. This strategy is part of the approach to learning used by the renowned physicist Richard Feynman, who would begin by writing what he knows about a subject as if he were teaching it to a sixth grader.

Also, sharing your reflections can be a self-imposed way to make sure you reflect in the first place. You can schedule a regular event in which you share reflections with others, like a colleague or friend. Creating a stable structure for that shared reflection can contribute to establishing and sustaining your reflective practice. You can also choose a set of prompts you always answer, a medium like a shared text document or a limited length or duration for your sharing.

Prompts

Prompts are jumping-off points that give your reflection momentum and direction. Now that you have tried the methods in the book, I've distilled them into prompts that you can incorporate into your pensieve to spark reflection for different purposes.

PROMPTS

If you want to add texture and depth to your perception of the world:

What mood am I in right now and how might it affect this [project/relationship]? What beliefs are beneath that mood? And what productive moods could I cultivate? (Experiment #1)

Where can I insert a moment of pause in this [project/day/week]? (Experiment #2)

Where is my attention focused right now? How could I adopt a different vantage point from which to see this [relationship/situation/problem/opportunity]? (Experiment #3)

If you want to better understand your interactions with others:

How might my identities play out in how I'm seeing or being seen as part of this [project/relationship/situation]? (Experiment #4)

If you want to make sense of situations you find yourself in:

What connections am I not seeing? How can I make those visible? (Experiment #5)

What kinds of questions should I be asking here? (Experiment #6)

If I achieve my goal, what would that do for me? How else could I achieve that goal? (Experiment #7)

Am I thinking inside a bubble? How can I create a hole in it and make new connections? (Experiment #8)

If you want to expand what's possible for a project or idea:

What could be the intended and unintended consequences of this [project/goal/action/trend]? (Experiment #9)

How can I make this idea/future tangible for myself and for other people? (Experiment #10)

How could I stretch the time horizon for this project? (Experiment #11)

How could the actions I'm taking now affect future generations? What alternative actions should I take to be a good ancestor? (Experiment #12)

In addition, these are general-purpose prompts that work very well across many situations:

I used to think . . . And now I think . . .: There is nothing more full of opportunity than those moments when you change your mind about something. Use this prompt to discover those moments.

I like . . . I wish . . . I wonder . . .: Use this prompt to quickly capture the benefits, the opportunities for improvement, and the questions that arise from an experience.

What? So what? Now what? This prompt efficiently encapsulates the premise of this book: What did you notice? What sense could you make of that? What are you going to do next?

In her book, *Creative Acts for Curious People*, Sarah Stein Greenberg expands on how these general-purpose prompts have been used across d.school courses to foster reflection in learning and suggests a few ways in which you can put them into practice.

Once you are done assembling your own pensieve, consider it an experiment to revisit regularly.

As I was writing this book, I created and refined a pensieve to use as reflection bookends for my day. You can see it on the following page. I fill my pensieve out first thing in the morning. It takes me less than five minutes, and it helps me set the tone for the day. In the evening I take a couple of minutes to revisit what I wrote in the morning and jot a few additional notes. Adding to the last section, "Sleep on It," I nudge my brain to dwell on any experience or lingering question overnight. I may also circle an insight or two to share with others the next day.

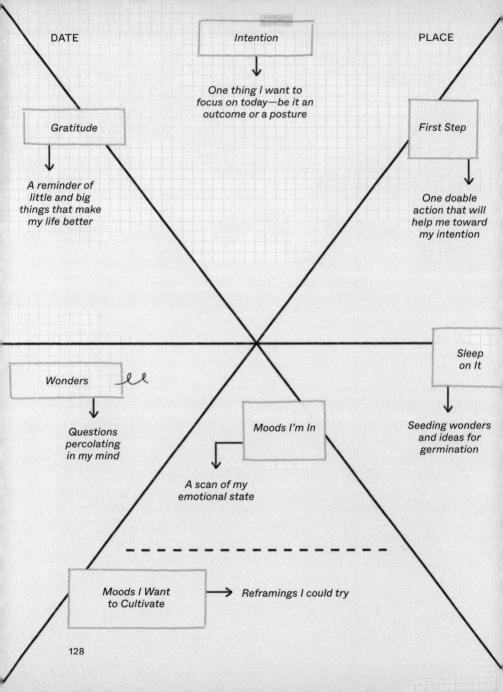

DATE

PLACE

Intention

One thing I want to
focus on today—be it an
outcome or a posture

Gratitude

A reminder of
little and big
things that make
my life better

First Step

One doable
action that will
help me toward
my intention

*Sleep
on It*

Wonders

Questions
percolating
in my mind

Moods I'm In

Seeding wonders
and ideas for
germination

A scan of my
emotional state

*Moods I Want
to Cultivate*

→ *Reframings I could try*

An Insight-o-Meter Logbook

In the introduction I shared the idea of using the insight-o-meter (see page 8) as a way to assess the results of your experiments. The insight-o-meter had you rate your experiments as *Meh, Hmm . . . , and Aha!*

How many of the experiments scored high on the insight-o-meter for you? While getting a life-changing insight will not happen every time you reflect, building a reflective practice drastically ups the odds in your favor. Also, insights tend to morph and recombine, and the more you gather, the more chances you create for that to happen. I encourage you to keep a logbook to take stock of your results across all experiments, and to go over your notes as a way to build your reflective muscle.

Here is a piece of advice I want to leave you with about what to do with your insights—whether they are in the *Aha!* territory or not yet there: treat them as new hypotheses to test through experimentation. That way they turn into stepping-stones that extend your learning journey.

Through this collection of experiments, I've offered you concrete methods you can add to your toolkit and use to build a reflective practice. My hope is that you go beyond that. Don't just *do* reflection. Embrace reflection as a way of *being*, and unlock new ways of seeing, making meaning, and shaping futures.

Sources and Resources

A source is the origin of something. A resource is a supply that can be tapped into or a strategy that can be adopted. For a list of sources and resources for this book, please visit **dschool.stanford.edu/books/reflection**. The sources section lists the origins of concepts and research findings mentioned throughout. The resources section unlocks inspiration and areas of exploration that extend from— and beyond—what I've included here. It contains materials that can be read, watched, listened to, and experienced, including bonus materials created for this book.

Grateful Reflections

The very first time I biked over from the biosciences building and stepped into the d.school, I knew I had found my place. And I never left. I'm fortunate to be surrounded by the kindest, quirkiest, and most collaborative group of people—across all teams and functions—who help create possibilities for me to grow and have impact. This book is one of those possibilities realized.

I've been lucky to teach with and learn from incredibly talented and caring educators. They have helped to shape my pedagogical beliefs and practices, which have permeated this book. Bre Przestrzelski, Carissa Carter, Dave Johnson, Frederik Pferdt, Guillermo Goyenola, Ilya Avdeev, Lonny Grafman, Maureen Carroll, Melissa Pelochino, Rodrigo Roncio, sam seidel, Silvia Umpiérrez Oroño, Susana Vieira, Tim Moore, Tina Seelig, Vivian Cuns: you all have been the best fellow experimenters I could have asked for. Coconspirators Erica Estrada-Liou and Meenu Singh nurture my creativity day in and day out, and our long-standing collaboration has inspired key concepts and tools included here, like the insight-o-meter.

I owe boundless gratitude to the students and University Innovation Fellows—too many to name—whom I've had the honor to serve.

Adapting reflection methods as experiments that can work in book format was a challenge that stretched me. The friends and colleagues who accepted my invitation to join the Reflection Lab were instrumental in testing and refining these reflection experiments. Thanks to Angélica Cuevas, Brian Malott, Brigitte Lundin, Daniel Burkholder, Dean Chang, Felipe Wilson, Glenn Fajardo, Grace Lin, Guy Williams, Hesam Panahi, Ilya Avdeev, Ingvi Ómarsson, Jason "TOGA" Trew, Jessica Aldrich, Joe Samosky, Joe Tranquillo, KC Christopher, Laurie Moore, Mary Raber, Natalie Fletcher, Paola Mera, Portia Buchongo, Ryan "Merlin" Middleton, Ryan Phillips, and Sedi Worlanyo.

My exploration of what reflection looks like in practice included conversations with many inspiring people: Alexandra Seda, Ariam Mogos, Ashanti Branch, Barry Svigals, Courtlandt Butts, Gloria Flores, Hakan Seyalioglu, Jeremy Utley, Kathryn Hymes, Keston Fulcher, Kwamou Eva Feukeu, Lauren Kunze, Louie Montoya, Meredith Hutchison, Neeraj Sonalkar, Rebecca Stockley, Seamus Yu Harte, Steve Seidel, and Tania Anaissie. There isn't enough space in this little book for all of their stories, but they invariably contributed to my learning.

My brilliant colleagues Charlotte Burgess-Auburn and Scott Doorley spearheaded the vision and implementation of the series this book belongs to. Along with the wonderful Jenn Brown, they made writing the book quite an adventure— from the fuzzy early phases to the most fun discussions about using this word or that word to convey a meaning or elicit a feeling. And then I lucked out when I found fellow

Uruguayan Gabriela Sánchez. Her art illustrates how reflection scratches beneath the surface of reality to expose the magic of possibility. My deep appreciation goes to my father and my aunts Cristina and Rosario for digging up old family photos to incorporate in a few of Gabriela's art pieces. Julie Bennett, Emma Campion, and the whole Ten Speed Press team were instrumental in bringing the book to life. I can't thank you enough for the incredible amount of meticulous work this took.

When I reflect further back in time, I am grateful to the people who have always been there for me, even when miles away: my whole family in Uruguay and my dear friend Nella. My deep appreciation goes to the teachers who taught me much more than what they could imagine: Mario Martinez taught me that basketball—like any other endeavor—is just an excuse to work on becoming a better person; Mónica Marin and Lucy Shapiro taught me the foundations of experimental thinking that have shaped my life well beyond the lab.

Reflecting forward, I thank you, the reader, for accepting this invitation to learn by experimenting.

I dedicate this book to my parents, Sarah and Fernando, who encouraged me to follow my curiosity and celebrated my experiments since as far back as I can remember. And I don't think I'll ever stop experimenting, so I thank my husband, Roy, who will be putting up with my crazy ideas when we are eighty years old, as he has been patiently doing for over a decade now.

Index

A

abstraction, exploring levels of, 71–77
Aldrich, Jessica, 120
ancestor, becoming a good, 115–21
Anders, William, 36–37
Apollo 8, 36–37
attention, broadening definition of, 31–39
Avdeev, Ilya, 83

B

Bambino, Debbie, 45
Barrett, Lisa Feldman, 18
beliefs, 19, 21
Borman, Frank, 36–37
Branch, Ashanti, 47
Brand, Stewart, 107
Buchongo, Portia, 47
Burks, Bea Karol, 120
Butts, Courtlandt, 45, 46

C

Carter, Carissa, 61
Clock of the Long Now, 109
commitments, eliminating, 28
context, changing, 39

D

dates, writing, 113
Dweck, Carol, 46

E

Edwards, Betty, 38
emotional granularity, 18
empty chair technique, 121
Eno, Brian, 107
Estrada-Liou, Erica, 57, 83
Ever Forward Club, 47
Experimenter's Pledge, 10–11
experiments
    anatomy of, 6, 8–9

"failed," 11
norms for, 10–11
power of, 1–2
private, 5
time length of, 5
tools needed for, 5
eyes, closing, 38

F

Feynman, Richard, 125
Flores, Gloria, 20
frameworks, 58, 59, 61
future generations
    connecting with, 115–21
    planting seeds for, 106, 108–9
futures
    artifacts from, 97–103
    imagining possible, 90–95, 98
    literacy, 90
    prospecting, 93, 106
    shaping, 4
    wheel, 93–95

G

Glenn, Jerome C., 93

H

Hayakawa, S. I., 75
Hillis, Danny, 107
Huang, Karen, 69
Hutchison, Meredith, 35

I

identities
    exploring, 41–49
    limiting, 46
incubation periods, 29
insight-o-meter
    logbook, 129
    using, 8–9
Institute for the Future, 101–2

J

Juliana, Kelsey, 116
Juliana v. United States, 116, 120

K

Knuth, Don, 76
Krznaric, Roman, 106, 119

L

Laidley, Debbi, 45
Langer, Ellen, 35
Long Now Foundation, 107, 113
Lovell, James, 36–37
Lundin, Brigitte, 45

M

McIntyre, Debbie, 45
metaphors, creating, 79–85
Middleton, Ryan, 60
mindset, fixed vs. growth, 46
Montoya, Louie, 119
moods
    beliefs underlying, 19, 21
    emotions vs., 16
    noticing, 15–21
    productive and unproductive, 18–20
Moon, Jenny, 122
Moore, Laurie, 36

P

Pace Layers model, 109–12
Paseo Protocol, 45
pensieve, building, 122–28
perspectives, contrasting, 39
Phillips, Ryan, 49
Poole, Robert, 37
preflection, 124
proflection, 90, 94
prompts, 125–27
prototyping, 99, 102

Q

Quate, Stevi, 45
questions
    asking, 63–69
    types of, 67–68
Quinn, Juli, 45

R

reflection
    definition of, 3–4
    forward, 89–95
    as habit, 122, 124
    imagination and, 87
    medium for, 124–25
    prompts for, 125–27
    sharing, 125
    tactile, 7
    timing and frequency of, 124
    as tool of awareness, 13
    types of, 90
Roth, Bernie, 72

S

Salk, Jonas, 116
Saltmarshe, Ella, 120
Samosky, Joseph, 100–101
Schön, Donald, 90
Seda, Alexandra, 102
seidel, sam, 10, 64
slowing down, 23–29
Solomon, Lisa Kay, 90
starting vs. finishing, 105–13
Stein Greenberg, Sarah, 127
Svigals, Barry, 64

T

thinking
    divergent, 75–77
    externalizing, 53–61
    long-term, 106, 112, 116
time horizons, reflecting on, 87,
    105–13
to-do list, assessing, 28
turning upside-down, 38

V

vantage point, moving, 36–37

W

waiting, tech-free, 39
Wilson, Felipe, 45–46

Z

zooming in and out, 36

Published in the United States by Ten Speed Press, an imprint of
Random House, a division of Penguin Random House LLC, New York.
TenSpeedPress.com

Ten Speed Press and the Ten Speed Press colophon are registered trademarks
of Penguin Random House LLC.

Family photos used in the art pieces on pages viii, 64, 70, 114, and 120 were
provided by Fernando Britos, Cristina Cavagnaro, and Rosario Cavagnaro.
The photo used in the art piece on page 40 was taken by David Puig.

Typefaces: Hope Meng's d.sign, Dinamo's Whyte and ABC Whyte Inktrap,
and Monotype's Cotford

Library of Congress Cataloging-in-Publication Data
Names: Cavagnaro, Leticia Britos, author.
Title: Experiments in reflection : how to see the present, reconsider
   the past, and shape the future / Leticia Britos Cavagnaro ; illustrations
   by Gabriela Sanchez.
Description: California : Ten Speed Press, [2023] | Includes bibliographical
   references and index.
Identifiers: LCCN 2022011656 (print) | LCCN 2022011657 (ebook) |
   ISBN 9781984858108 (trade paperback) | ISBN 9781984858115 (ebook)
Subjects: LCSH: Insight. | Introspection. | Awareness. | Self-realization.
Classification: LCC BF449.5 .C38 2023 (print) | LCC BF449.5 (ebook) |
   DDC 153.4—dc23/eng/20220914
LC record available at https://lccn.loc.gov/2022011656
LC ebook record available at https://lccn.loc.gov/2022011657

Trade Paperback ISBN: 978-1-9848-5810-8
eBook ISBN: 978-1-9848-5811-5

Printed in China

Acquiring editor: Hannah Rahill | Project editor: Julie Bennett
Designer: Emma Campion | Production designer: Mari Gill
Production editor: Sohayla Farman
Production and prepress color manager: Jane Chinn
Copyeditor: Kristi Hein | Proofreader: Lisa Brousseau | Indexer: Ken DellaPenta
Publicist: Kate Tyler | Marketer: Chloe Aryeh
d.school creative team: Jennifer Brown, Charlotte Burgess-Auburn, and Scott Doorley

10 9 8 7 6 5 4 3 2 1

First Edition